walking meditations

To my friends Pushan and Kasia.
May you continue to lovingly walk this path
together for many lifetimes.

An Hachette UK Company
www.hachette.co.uk

First published in Great Britain
in 2023 by Aster, an imprint of
Octopus Publishing Group Ltd
Carmelite House,
50 Victoria Embankment,
London EC4Y 0DZ
www.octopusbooks.co.uk

Text copyright © Danielle North 2023
Illustrations copyright © SpaceFrog Designs
2023

Distributed in the US by
Hachette Book Group
1290 Avenue of the Americas,
4th and 5th Floors, New York,
NY 10104

Distributed in Canada by
Canadian Manda Group
664 Annette Street, Toronto,
Ontario, Canada M6S 2C8

ISBN 978 1 78325 562 7

A CIP catalogue record for this book
is available from the British Library.
Printed and bound in China.

10 9 8 7 6 5 4 3 2 1

Commissioning Editor: Nicola Crane
Art Director: Yasia Williams
Illustrators: SpaceFrog Designs
Senior Editor: Alex Stetter
Copy Editor: Caroline West
Production Managers: Lucy Carter & Nic Jones

walking meditations

To find a place of peace, wherever you are

Danielle North

ASTER*

Contents

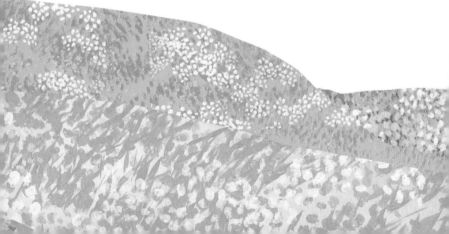

Part 1
A World of Walking

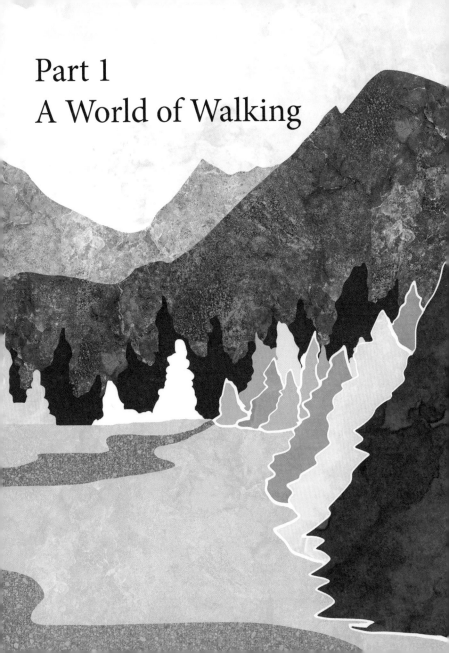

The cosmos moves in cycles and rhythms on a scale way beyond our human understanding of size and time. We are part of this magnificent universe and moved in mysterious ways by it. Long ago, our ancestors would have been attuned to these natural rhythms, gazing at the vast night sky and using the planets and stars for guidance on how to live their lives. Today, it has become harder for us to attune even to earthly rhythms, such as the changes in the seasons, and so we give little or no thought to the bigger cycles occurring in space that are also guiding and supporting us.

One of the reasons we have lost touch with this bigger context is that modern living can be a bumpy experience. From birth through schooling, the world of work, parenting and beyond, few people escape the inevitable knocks and bruises to heart and soul along the way. The result of this is that we are often operating with our heads down and blinkers on, as we focus on getting through daily challenges or the next stressful situation that life seems to throw our way.

This is where walking comes in. When we have experienced challenges, difficulties or even trauma in our lives, the repetitive and steady rhythm of putting one foot in front of the other, connecting to the earth below and to our own selves, is a restorative and healing process. If you can walk in nature, or places that have spiritual significance (along ley lines, for example), these benefits are amplified.

Walks don't need to be long to be meaningful. A short, ten-minute walk, a 'scene-changer', can often be enough to break your state, helping to restore balance and regulate the central nervous system. Over time, the benefits of regular walking mean that you can re-pattern the brain to create new neural networks, so that walking becomes not only a habit, but also something that increases your feelings of well-being, peace and happiness.

Longer walks, such as the Seasonal Meditations on pages 136–159, are a chance for us to get lost along the way, either by going off the beaten track and exploring new locations, or simply by getting lost within ourselves, in our own thoughts or experiences. When so much of life is lived according to a schedule, dealing with other people's demands, there is rarely space for surprises. Yet in the emptiness of space there are unknowns, insights and answers waiting to be discovered. There is also a section on Deeper Meditations (see pages 126–135), containing step-by-step walking meditations designed to take you even further and provide you with guidance if you are experiencing especially complex, powerful or difficult emotions.

This book has been written to guide you on a meditative journey when walking, combining the benefits of walking and meditation. It may be useful to download the audio version of this book, so that you can listen to the meditations as you walk. You may also want to think about a place where you can walk regularly; a location that is easy and convenient for you to reach from home or your workplace.

The meditations in this book are for anyone who wants to feel the benefits of meditation but finds the idea or experience of sitting still to meditate too challenging. They are also for those who already have a meditation practice and want to take it beyond sitting on a cushion daily or relying on a meditation app. Ultimately, the goal is to be able to cultivate the sensation and benefits of walking meditation as we go about our day-to-day activities, so we can feel less stressed and more peaceful every day.

For now, let's enjoy exploring the positive benefits of walking meditation together, using the rhythm of walking and focusing on breathing as a way to connect with our inner world. Over time, perhaps walking meditation will also help you find a way to reconnect with those mysterious and life-sustaining rhythms of the cosmos…

Galaxies of love,
Danielle x

Why walking works

Walking is one of the most accessible and pleasurable forms of exercise you can take throughout your life. If done regularly, it benefits both your physical and mental health. Walking alleviates depression; increases energy; improves your mood; reduces stress and anxiety; and enhances the quality of your sleep. These benefits are amplified when you walk in nature, and the nourishment gained from being outdoors also creates a deep feeling of calm within. As you disconnect from the stresses and strains of everyday life, you connect with the restorative power of nature and build a deeper connection with yourself.

Research into the Japanese practice of *Shinrin-yoku*, or 'forest bathing', shows that spending time among trees, being calm and breathing deeply, improves mood and reduces anxiety. The energy that sustains the earth also sustains you. In some traditions, this life-force energy is known as qi or chi (Chinese), ki (Japanese) or prana (Sanskrit). You may not be conscious that this life force is being activated as you walk in nature, but you will feel its benefits. This is the same energy that is cultivated when people sit in meditation. As people meditate, qi begins to rise, and so walking in nature is essentially a form of meditation.

If you use the meditations in this book over time and with awareness, you may be able to feel this life-force energy rising within you and even cultivate it. As your life force rises, so too does your own natural energy, motivation and zest for life, along with your ability to feel more grounded and clear-headed.

What is walking meditation?

Meditation continues to grow in popularity around the globe. Usually when people think of meditation, they picture someone sitting very still, in silence on a cushion, with their back straight and hands in their lap, and with a quiet, empty mind for a period of time. While this is a powerful way to develop concentration, tranquility and insight, for many of us with busy lives and even busier minds, meditating in this way simply feels out of reach.

Even those who manage to sit on a meditation cushion often think they are doing it wrong because they are unable to experience a quiet mind. In truth, the mind is rarely quiet, especially when we are learning to meditate, and the aim to begin with is simply to observe the breath rather than silence the mind. As our meditation practice develops, we become more able to detach from our thoughts and simply observe them. You can discover more about how to meditate in this way in my other books, *Sleep Meditations* and *Morning Meditations*.

Throughout this book you will learn how to practise meditating as you walk, which is essentially very simple. The meditations are inspired by the Zen walking meditation practice known as *Kinhin*. However, you don't need to be a Buddhist to practise this form of meditation. Walking meditation combines the ability to focus the mind with purposeful focused movement, so you can expand the natural stress-reducing benefits of walking without any additional effort.

How does walking meditation work?

Traditional walking meditation practice is done slowly and barefoot, with the gaze lowered. Your hands can be clasped lightly in front or behind you, or you can let your arms hang loosely by your sides. You walk a specific number of paces – for example, fifteen paces – along a set path. The aim is to coordinate your breathing with the steps you take, so walk nice and slowly. At the end of the path, you pause, turn around and walk the same number of paces back. As you return to your starting point, you pause again, then walk back along the path, and so on. During this meditation, the intention is to focus your attention on the sensations in your feet. And that is all: a complete and mindful connection with the soles of your feet. At the beginning, middle and end of the path, you can ask 'Where is my mind?' in order to bring your attention back to the sensations in the soles of your feet.

This approach to meditation works because the mind wants something on which to focus. If you give the mind a point of focus to concentrate on, you will know if it has wandered off and you can refocus without judgement. All you need to do is bring your attention back to the soles of your feet while maintaining a mindful walking pace. This is particularly beneficial if you are new to meditation, as it provides you with natural check-in points. Observing the mind in action is powerful because the more you practise this skill, the more you understand and experience that you have a mind, but you are not only your mind – you and your mind are separate entities.

Using this book while walking

Each meditation in this book has been written with a particular intention in mind. Some are deliberately short, for those days when you are snatching some time for yourself, but there are also deeper meditations for processing complex emotions (see pages 126–135) and extended meditations for times of seasonal transition (see pages 136–159).

You can incorporate the meditations in your day, and 'stack' them with existing routines, such as returning from the school run, on your lunch break or going to the gym. It won't always be possible to go barefoot for these meditations, but that's okay; you can still pay attention to the sensations in your feet through your shoes.

There may be moments when you want to sit and reflect. If time allows, this is to be encouraged, and you can either sit quietly with your thoughts or focus on your breathing. This can be particularly helpful with the longer meditations, as you can take this book with you and read the next section. For the shorter ones, spend a moment reading the meditation before you leave the house. Don't worry about trying to remember the meditation for the whole journey, as you can make it your own as you are walking. You can, of course, download the audio version of the book and listen to one of these as you walk instead.

If walking is difficult for you, you can read or listen to the meditations and take the journey in your imagination. If you are able to do this outside, that will further enhance the benefits.

Getting Started

Walking with awareness

Walking meditation is simply walking and breathing with awareness. If you want to get started in a simple way, here are seven ideas to help you to walk with awareness:

1. Observe as many different shades and tones of green as possible.
2. Walk where there is space. Deliberately find the space between people and things.
3. Look for, and if you can do so safely, touch as many different textures as you can.
4. Bring awareness to everything you can smell – what do you like and dislike?
5. Listen to the sound of your own breathing as you walk. No more, no less.
6. Observe what is natural and what is man-made.
7. Look for beauty, in everything. Even if it is not there.

Breathwork for walking

In walking meditation, you focus on coordinating your breathing with the rhythm of your steps. Since you were born, you have been breathing. It happens naturally without you thinking about it, approximately 1,000 times an hour, and for many of us, it happens with ease. So, given this is such a natural human process, why do we need to pay attention to it during our walking meditations?

Modern living can be stressful and prolonged periods of stress mean the sympathetic nervous system activates the fight-or-flight response with a sudden rush of hormones, including the stress hormone cortisol, into the body. You feel alert, your heartbeat and breathing quickens, and your body tenses up. When the stress has passed, the parasympathetic nervous system restores the body to a state of calm. For many of us, modern living activates the sympathetic nervous system and our cortisol levels become elevated for too long, creating a hormonal imbalance that makes it difficult to switch off.

By making conscious changes to your breathing patterns, the vagus nerve, which runs from the brain to the diaphragm, sends a signal to your brain to turn up your parasympathetic nervous system and turn down your sympathetic nervous system. When the parasympathetic system is activated, your breathing slows, your heart rate drops, your blood pressure lowers, and your body is put into a state of calm.

It's like a light switch that you can flick to change how you feel, and you do this simply by taking a deep breath or changing your breathing pattern. To help you reset your system, you can either use these simple breathing techniques as you walk – that will be your walking meditation – or you can practise them seated at home when you want to give your energy a boost.

Conscious breathing is a breath in through your nose, down into your belly and out through your mouth. The out-breath is like a soft sigh – imagine you are steaming up a bathroom mirror as you exhale. Continue breathing in this way for a few more steps, harmonizing your inhale and exhale with the pace of your steps.

Balanced breathing is a practice in which you only breathe through your nose. Close your mouth and inhale slowly through your nose (both nostrils) for a count of 4 and then exhale slowly through your nose for a count of 4. Connect the rhythm of your breathing to the rhythm of your walking. Repeat the cycle five times. It can help to use your right hand to count the breaths and your left hand to count the cycles. Keep your hands relaxed by your sides as you count, so you don't tense your body.

Spiral breathing is an opportunity to imagine your breath spiralling up and down your spine as you walk. Take a deep breath in and, as you inhale, allow your breath to spiral up your spine for a count of 6. As you exhale, let the breath naturally spiral back down your spine for a count of 6. If it helps, you can imagine the breath has a colour and watch this colour moving up and down your spine.

Step by step: Walking with your senses

Often when we are walking our attention is not grounded, as we're often listening to music or a podcast, speaking to friends or scrolling on our smartphone. Even when we walk in silence, it's easy to find the mind freewheeling with worries, doubts, frustrations or aspirations, desires and dreams. None of this is wrong, but to feel less stressed and more relaxed, try this practice of walking with the senses instead.

This practice works best when we disconnect from tech and walk alone (it's okay if there are other people around, though – for instance, in a busy street or supermarket). Here's how to do it:

Step 1 As you walk, slow down your pace.

Step 2 Relax your breathing.

Step 3 Observe what you can see in the foreground near you: textures, colours, patterns.

Step 4 Shift your attention to what you can see in the distance: textures, colours, patterns.

Step 5 Tune in to what you can hear, including sounds you like and sounds you don't like.

Step 6 Become aware of any smells and notice what you like and don't like.

Step 7 Notice if you can be with it all, just as it is.

Step 8 Breathing in and out as you walk.

Step 9 Now feel your centre, the core of you.

Step 10 Walk from your core, feeling strong and steady.

Ten-minute mood boost

If you are feeling depleted, this walking meditation can be done at home or while walking from one place to another; each part only takes a few minutes. If you are somewhere busy, start with Part 2, or practise just Part 2 if time is short. If you have more time, you can extend the number of rounds.

Part 1 Centre yourself
1. Start in a standing position.
2. Place your right hand over your heart.
3. Connect with your heart. Feel the steady beat of your heart.
4. Focus on your breathing.
5. Send your breath into the space beneath your hand.

Part 2 Breathe and feel
1. Release your hand and begin to walk slowly.
2. Breathe into your heart for a slow count of 5. Step by step.
3. Breathe out for a count of 5. Step by step.
4. Slowly and steadily for five rounds. Notice how you feel.
5. Make space for those feelings.

Part 3 Experience joy
1. Think of someone or something that brings you joy.
2. Notice how joy feels in your body.
3. Breathe joy into your heart. Breathe joy out into the world. 5 counts in and 5 counts out. Step by step. Slowly and steadily for five rounds.
4. Notice any shifts in your body and mind.

Going Deeper

The inner dimension

Much of our lives are spent with our attention and focus outside of ourselves, particularly when we are walking because we can do this on autopilot. When the mind has the freedom to wander to other matters, it can move in a myriad different directions at lightening speed, from creative thinking, to problem solving, to engaging with the world around us, or even to catastrophizing!

Meditation calls on us to make the journey into the world within. We all have an inner ocean, a vast landscape within us made up of our thoughts, feelings, values, attitudes and beliefs. This is also where our instincts, intuition and inner knowing reside. The walking meditations in this book are designed to help you discover your own inner dimensions, so you can know your true self and be kind to yourself and others along the way.

The art of contemplation

Even after all our attempts to understand the complexity of what it is to be human, we have only scratched the surface, and there are many hidden depths to be discovered, or rediscovered, that go beyond the logic of our minds. The art of contemplation allows us to go into these deeper places in our awareness, intuition and understanding of ourselves. Walking meditations are a route into this beautiful, deep, rich sea within.

Walking peacefully

Often, in our everyday lives, we are focused on getting somewhere. Take a moment and make a list of all the places you are trying to get to in a day, from physical locations like the train station and the supermarket, to aspirational ones such as achieving better health, a good relationship or a change of career. So much of our lives is focused on going somewhere, and when all our energy and focus is on the future and trying to be somewhere else, we can lose the feeling of peace that comes from being in the here and now.

To deepen your walking meditation practice and your ability to walk peacefully, rather than just incorporate it into a walk with a destination – perhaps a trip to the office or the gym – experiment with going on a walk that has no destination, so the purpose of the walk becomes the walk itself. As before, all you need to do is focus on walking and breathing (see page 20). Here's how to do it.

Step 1 Place one foot in front of the other and feel the sensation of your heel connecting to the ground.

Step 2 Become aware of your whole foot as it rolls forwards towards your toes and notice the heel lifting from the ground now as your other foot takes a step forwards.

Step 3 Breathe and notice, and stay in the present moment, knowing that there is nowhere else you need to be; you are just peacefully placing one foot in front of the other.

Effortless action

Having reached the guided meditations in the book, now is a good time to remember why we practice walking meditation at all. The main intention is to bring your practice beyond the walking meditation and into your daily life. To bring the peace you have cultivated in your walking meditations into your everyday life, so it will be useful in your work, relationships or parenting. Ultimately, the place of peace you find in your meditations becomes a continuous and connected space within you that is not separate. To do this, first it is necessary to practise, so use any opportunity you have to keep moving with consciousness, whether that is getting up from the sofa or taking a long hike in the mountains, until it no longer requires conscious thought and becomes effortless action.

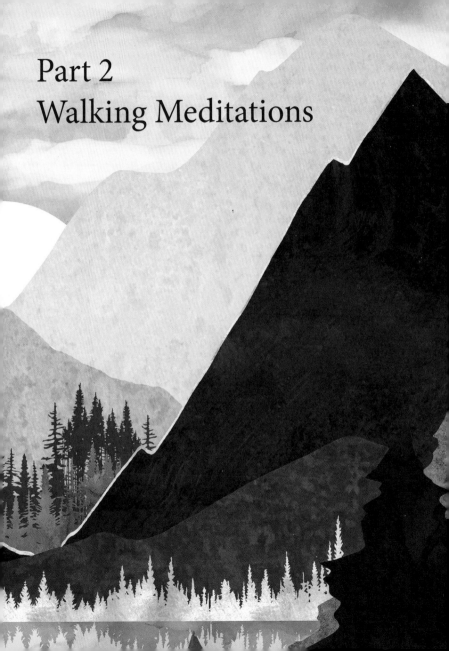

Part 2
Walking Meditations

Calm

Connect with your physical body as you walk and, on your next exhale, imagine gently blowing a trail of small, blue bubbles through your mouth. Breathe in and then visualize the stream of tiny, blue bubbles on the exhale. Repeat this in your own time for ten breaths.

Enjoy this moment, smile and be playful as you see the bubbles leave your body on the out-breath. Play with the colour blue – is it a dark midnight blue, a bright turquoise or a soft, pale blue? Find your colour or mix the blues together. Keep it light and playful and remember that this works best if you exhale through an open mouth.

Now look around at your surroundings. You may be in an urban landscape or perhaps out in the countryside. Wherever you are, begin to see trails of tiny, blue bubbles being exhaled by the people around you.

Everyone is breathing, inhaling and exhaling. The essentials of life. Inhale and exhale. It's that simple.

Pay attention now to any trees in your surroundings and visualize the trees exhaling tiny streams of gorgeous green bubbles.

See how expansive the trees are as they breathe and watch
the trails of bright emerald-green bubbles generously releasing
oxygen into the atmosphere. Picture every tree releasing enough
tiny, green bubbles to help each person on the planet to breathe.

Notice that the trees continue to
breathe freely, even if the conditions
are challenging – and so can you.

Watch as your bubbles and the trees' bubbles begin to overlap
and connect in a colourful kaleidoscopic constellation.
A myriad of blue and green bubbles mixed together.

We are connected to each other through this simple exchange
and everyone is connected to the life-giving air that we breathe.
We are one, and even amid the chaos, we continue to walk our
path and, with every breath we take – this essential of life – we
are well.

Gratitude

As you set off on your walk, take a deep breath in through your nose, hold it for just a moment and then exhale long and slow.

Take another deep breath in through your nose, hold for just a moment and then exhale long and slow.

One more time, inhale deeply, hold and exhale long and slow. Now return to your regular breathing, just as it is for you; there's no need to change it.

Imagine a soft golden light surrounding you. It shimmers and shines gently. You feel completely safe and protected, enveloped in this beautiful light.

Focus on your feet as they make contact with the ground and let the soft golden light begin to enter your feet, filling you with warmth and relaxation as you feel grateful to your feet for every step you have ever taken on this path in life, leading you to this moment, right here, right now.

Now feel the soft golden light begin to move up into your ankles. Feel your ankles become warm and relaxed, as this light begins to move up into your calves and shins.

Feel that soft golden light move into your knees, and let the warmth fill your knees and move up into your thighs. Pay attention to the big muscles in your thighs and, with every step you take, feel grateful for the strength you have in your body.

Now let the soft golden light move into your hip joints. Letting your hips soften and relax, gently swaying, step by step.

Become aware of the warm golden light filling your abdomen. Feel a ball of golden light filling your abdominal area. Feel the warmth from the ball of light. Take a deep breath into that ball of light and feel it expand, filling you with warmth and gratitude for being you.

With each breath you take, let your lungs fill with that soft golden light, expanding your gratitude for every single breath you have taken in this life – what a miraculous being you are!

Let your awareness move to your hands. Feel the warm golden light fill each finger. Feel it fill the palm of each hand, as you experience gratitude for your ability to touch, connect and create.

Let the golden light begin to move into your wrists and up your forearms, then flow into your upper arms and shoulders. Let your shoulder blades relax. Feeling deeply relaxed and grateful for all that you are able to hold on behalf of yourself and others.

Next, let the warm golden light enter your neck. Feel your neck and throat begin to relax. Swallow gently and feel your throat open.

Feel the light as it fills your entire head and face. Let your eyes relax. Allow that little space between your eyebrows to relax. Let your forehead relax. Let the top of your head relax.

Now feel the golden light flow up through the crown of your head and down the back of your body, like a warm glow bathing your spine, vertebrae by vertebrae. And feel grateful for your backbone that keeps you strong and true in life.

Smile and, with each step you take, enjoy feeling grateful to you for being alive, right here in this moment, right now.

Focus

As you put on your shoes, become aware of your physical body and make a connection with your feet. You can do this by rubbing the soles of your feet before you slip on your shoes.

If you need a coat, become aware of your arms entering the sleeves, and place your right hand on your left arm and your left hand on your right arm, giving yourself a squeeze or rubbing your arms to make contact with your physical body.

Feel the weight of your keys in your hand as you pick them up. Notice the temperature, sound and texture of your keys.

As you open the door, take a breath and become aware of how you feel today without judgement or the need to change how you are.

Carefully close the door and notice the shift
of energy as you exit your home and cross the
threshold into the outer world. How do you feel
about this change? Simply notice it, bringing
awareness to your experience in real time,
without needing to alter it.

Take a deep breath, in through your nose and
out through your mouth. You can do this two
or three times, if it feels good.

With every step you take, reconnect to your
feet and feel the energy as it transfers from
your feet and up into your body. Stay connected
to your breathing and notice that there is a short
pause between the in-breath and the out-breath.

Now, maintaining focus on your body and breathing, begin to turn your attention to the world around you. So often when we move into action, we lose connection with ourselves, with our being, and get lost in the doing.

Become aware of the subtle changes in you when you move to action. Does your belly constrict? Does your breathing become faster?

Simply notice with curiosity.
Stay focused on your own experience
as you engage with the external world
around you.

Continue this practice until you reach your destination or
return home. Remember that each time you do this, you
will have a different experience, which is all part of the fun!

Over time, the more you practise, the more capacity you
will have to focus on the everyday tasks at hand.

Energy

As you set off on your walk, imagine in your mind's eye that you are stepping out into a sunny day. Walking through grassland, you look up and the sky is blue, the sun warms your back, and you feel happy and content, knowing that this is a good day to be alive.

You pass through a gate and begin a gentle descent down the edge of a valley. In the distance, you hear a river singing happily as it meanders towards the ocean.

A stone wall marks the threshold and on the other side an undisturbed ancient oak woodland awaits you. There is a welcome and perceptible shift in temperature, and you become aware that the air feels cooler and damper here.

As you cross the threshold into the ancient woodland, you instantly feel an energy rise up through your body.

You become aware of an entirely different energy and aliveness here, as the extensive underground network that links the oak trees together, the wood-wide web, flourishes.

Each of the trees, young and old, communicates with the others beneath the ground, protecting each other and keeping them all healthy and safe.

Standing still for a moment, you sense this extraordinary giant superorganism and you plant your feet solidly on the ground beneath you, knowing that you are a part of it, that you have always been a part of it.

You send your roots deep into the earth, and then breathe the powerful earth energy as it flows up through your feet, past your ankles and knees, through your thighs and into your hips.

This earth energy gathers at your lower back and fills your abdomen.

You breathe deeply the air full of goodness and feel nourished from this powerful source of energy.

You raise your arms into the air, imagining you are like a mighty oak tree and feeling the energy rise up through your body and out towards the heavens through your fingertips. Yes, it is a good day to be alive!

Perspective

As you walk, instead of thinking about your tasks and to-do lists, talking on your smartphone or worrying about a situation, take a deep breath and focus your attention outside of you.

Allow your attention to zoom in on the tiny details you can see. A flower pushing its way through a crack in the concrete, for example. Focus in on all the small details of the world around you, perhaps dew drops on a spider's web like crystals on a silk thread or the patterns in the pavement.

Spend some time moving your attention from one small detail to the next, remembering to maintain a steady breathing pattern, inhaling and exhaling in an easy, natural way as you walk.

When you are ready, change your perspective and begin to zoom out to the bigger landscape around you.

Let your attention drift towards the skyline, pause and observe the sky and the clouds.

If you are in a built-up area, scan the tops of buildings, looking for patterns in the roof tiles and chimneys.

Be aware of undulation, layers and depth within the wider landscape.

As you walk, alternate your perspective between the micro and macro, each time savouring what you see in the ordinary, everyday aspects of life.

When you are ready, let go of it all and simply return to your breathing, moving step by step, feeling grounded and clear.

Creativity

Start by getting grounded as you walk, focusing on your feet and the stability you feel as they connect with the ground.

Now begin to tune in to what can you hear inside you – for example, your heartbeat or thoughts might be audible. Stay with your inner world for a few breaths.

Listen now to the sounds in your immediate vicinity; perhaps you can hear the refuse collectors, or the birds singing, rain falling or an emergency service siren. What sounds are in the space around you? Stay with the world around you for a few breaths.

Next, take a deep breath and begin
to open your ears to the sounds that
are beyond you.

These are sounds that exist, but you can't actively hear them.
Imagine worms burrowing underground, a field of bright red
poppies rustling in a soft breeze, tropical parrotfish scratching
at coral reefs, the chants of monks on a remote hillside temple,
giant sequoia trees drawing water up through their trunks.

Imagine tectonic plates moving against each other; a herd
of wildebeest stampeding across the great plains; snowdrops
gallantly pushing through the earth after a long, cold winter;
stars collapsing in the universe.

Be creative, stretch your imagination, and let yourself hear the sounds of the world you inhabit.

Flow

Picture yourself at an ornate archway, the entrance to a beautiful Japanese Zen garden. You hear the chime of a bell, a call from inside, and you enter this sacred space feeling a gentle shift in energy as you cross the threshold.

As you walk, imagine the delicate crunch of gravel underfoot, and from this moment on, let each step you take feel as light as a butterfly.

Bring awareness to the space between your feet and the ground beneath you as you tread lightly in this peaceful place.

Either side of the pathway, large, grey, mottled rocks mark the way and guide you on this meditative journey, as you feel a light moisture in the air that gently touches your skin.

You are drawn towards the tinkling sound of water. You follow the sound, arriving at a small waterfall where tiny drops of water, like sparking crystals, bounce off the rocks as the water flows towards a beautiful still lake.

Your attention is drawn to the still water of the lake, and you stop and gaze at the peace and beauty here.

As you look towards the centre of the lake, you notice some koi, which start to swim towards you. Each koi is like its own work of art. You see that one is pure yellow. Another glides by, its white body splashed with deep red patches overlaid with splashes of black and its white tail gently moving from left to right.

Another koi swims past with golden scales shimmering in the sunlight; you notice every scale has a black outline, making them stand out in full beauty.

An orange koi with black banding lifts its head towards the surface, and you notice that your pace has slowed, your breathing has settled, and you feel a sense of calm wash over you.

You continue to walk, crossing a bridge to a quiet place deep within the garden. Here the space is sheltered by trees and you can hear leaves rustling gently in the breeze.

Sitting on a flat rock in the centre of this space is your teacher or guide. Someone who has your best interests at heart. You have come to be here with them.

As you approach your guide, they stand and smile to greet you. They have nothing but love in their eyes and without words you begin to walk together.

After a while you say to your guide, 'I have come to you, what would you like me to know?'

Your guide says your name and begins to speak, sharing the wisdom that will be helpful for you to flow with ease in your life, like the koi.

You listen to what your guide has to say and allow the dialogue to flow. You are able to ask your guide questions and receive their answers with an open heart and good grace. You feel alive and awake.

Eventually, you find yourself back at the ornate archway, and it is time for you and your guide to part company. You do so with a quiet appreciation and deep love.

Clarity

As you walk, begin by fully exhaling through your open mouth for one breath, then take a nice big breath in and fully exhale out through your open mouth with a long, deep sigh – this resets your natural breathing pattern.

Now let your breath return to normal and, as you breathe normally, become aware of your breath and where it naturally wants to go in your body.

Follow the journey of your breath. Does it reach your chest? Does it fill your side ribs? Does the breath make its way down into your belly?

With every inhale simply notice and be curious about where your breath wants to go without trying to change it or judge it.

Now let that exploration go and turn your attention to your face. Noticing how you feel around your eyes, becoming aware of how you feel in your jaw and paying attention to your throat.

Take a deep breath in now and, on the exhale, let go of any tension in your face. Exhaling tension from around your eyes, breathing out any tension in your jaw. On the next exhale, softening your throat.

Next become aware of your shoulders. Take a deep breath in and, on the next exhale, let go of any tension in your shoulders.

As you become aware of your stomach now, taking a deep breath in and, on the next exhale, letting go of any tension and softening your stomach.

Focus on your legs now, breathing in deeply, and on the next exhale, let go of any tension in your legs, so that as you walk you begin to feel more relaxed than you have all day.

Finally, take a deep breath in, the most beautiful breath you've taken all day, and on the next exhale, sigh it all out, just as you did at the start of this walk.

Now your focus moves to counting your breath. On the next breath, your exhale is going to be 2 counts longer than your inhale. So, as you inhale, you might count to 4 and then, as you exhale, you might count to 6. Just find the count that feels most comfortable for you.

Inhale for 1, 2, 3, 4, exhale for 1, 2, 3, 4, 5, 6.

Inhale for 1, 2, 3, 4, exhale for 1, 2, 3, 4, 5, 6.

Inhale for 1, 2, 3, 4, exhale for 1, 2, 3, 4, 5, 6.

Each person's breath is different, so experiment with the count that suits you and find your own rhythm. You can't get this wrong, as everybody is different; it's just counting and breathing.

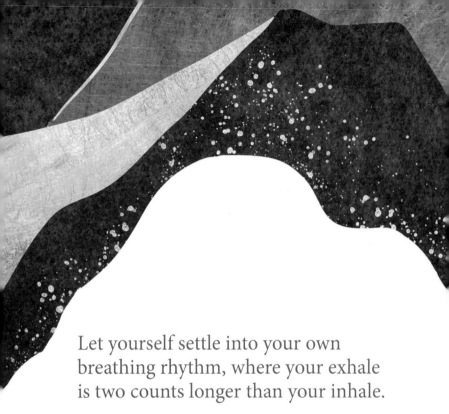

Let yourself settle into your own breathing rhythm, where your exhale is two counts longer than your inhale.

Now, if you can, you're going to add a pause at the top of your inhale, so that you pause for a second before you exhale and, again at the bottom, pause for a second before your inhale. So, you inhale for 4, pause, then exhale for 6, and pause. Like this:

Inhale for 1, 2, 3, 4, pause, exhale for 1, 2, 3, 4, 5, 6, pause.

Inhale for 1, 2, 3, 4, pause, exhale for 1, 2, 3, 4, 5, 6, pause.

Inhale for 1, 2, 3, 4, pause, exhale for 1, 2, 3, 4, 5, 6, pause.

Now you're going to return to a normal breath. No counts, no longer exhales, no pauses; just letting your breath do what it naturally does and noticing how you feel now.

Peace

In your mind's eye, picture a white dove in the blue sky above you. A symbol of purity and peace. As you walk and settle into your natural rhythm, the dove transforms into a small, bright white light, just hovering in front of your nose.

With each step you take, your breath naturally enters your body and the white light follows your breath. A pure white light fills your body with peace and calm. As your breath naturally leaves your body, you feel the pure white light expanding the peace and calm within you.

Breathing in pure white light, filling you with peace and calm.

Breathing out pure white light, expanding peace and calm.

Breathing in pure white light, filling you with peace and calm.

Breathing out pure white light, expanding peace and calm.

Breathing in pure white light, filling you with peace and calm.

Breathing out pure white light, expanding peace and calm.

The white light returns to hovering in front of your nose, then, on the next exhale, watch as this light expands and turns into a flock of doves. Each dove a symbol of peace, flying off into the bright blue sky.

Become aware of your feet and, as each foot touches the ground, feel a strong and powerful sense of peace and calm rising up from the earth beneath you. You feel wonderfully peaceful, safe and calm and know that you can return to this place of peace whenever you choose.

Strength

You are going on a journey. It is a journey back to you, a journey to rediscover the strength that resides deep within you.

If you ever feel lost along the way, simply come back to your breath; nothing else is required, no effort is needed here.

Imagine you are standing at the top of a magnificent stone staircase. As you begin your journey, each step leads you down this staircase.

You take the first step and count down slowly with every step from 10, knowing that you are completely safe and secure, 9, 8, 7, 6.

With every step, you feel calm and relaxed. Step 5, even more deeply relaxed; 4, deeper now; 3, relaxing further; 2, almost floating now; and 1, as you arrive at a beautiful garden.

The garden is infused with a peaceful and radiant light, and every part of your body and being feels completely comfortable and at ease.

You are surrounded by beauty and nature, and you gaze in awe at the living beauty of your surroundings.

As you walk through the garden, you draw strength with every step from the sights of the trees and sounds of the birds and scents of the flowers.

It is a place where you know you can cultivate and grow strength. A place where strength cannot help but enter you.

You reach a place where the ground is bare and a small, red and yellow bird flies down and lands on the ground.

The bird drops five golden seeds from its beak and gracefully takes flight. You know this is a gift for you, and you place the golden seeds in the palm of your right hand, closing your hand and resting it gently over your heart.

Your heart is strong and good, and you pour your heart's deepest wishes into the seeds before planting them, one at a time, in the fresh earth, knowing that these loving intentions will grow stronger over time.

You spend as much time as you need here, filling yourself up with all the goodness this place has to give.

When you are ready, feeling strong and steady, you return to the stone staircase and begin to count the steps as you climb – 1, 2, 3, 4, 5, becoming more aware of your physical body as you walk; 7, 8, becoming more aware of your breathing now; 9, 10, becoming aware of your feet as they connect with the ground beneath you.

Being

This is a meditation for just being; everything is done with ease and without outcome. Your arms hang lightly by your sides, your breath is easy and your gaze soft.

All you need to do is place one foot in front of the other, starting with your right foot. As you do so, feel the sensation of your heel connecting to the ground, become aware of your whole foot as it rolls forwards towards your toes, and notice the heel lifting from the ground as your left foot naturally moves forwards.

Breathe and notice, and stay in the present moment, knowing there is nowhere else you need to be – you are just peacefully placing one foot in front of the other.

As you walk, connect to a place of stillness within, and
from this place of stillness silently say these words to yourself
until you feel complete:

I am on my own, but I am not alone.

I am elemental.

The earth, air, ocean and sun are
within me.

Grounding

As you set off on your walk, visualize yourself walking along a path through an alpine meadow of wild flowers.

Standing proudly in the distance, dominating the skyline, are majestic mountain peaks; the base of the mountains is protected by a cool, restful pine forest. The winter snow has melted and is now sweeping down the mountainsides and pouring life into the earth, from which nature's alchemy has created an astounding display of colourful wild flowers.

The meadow is like a spectacular painting, bursting with vitality
as wild flowers of every colour sway in the gentle breeze. Purple
alpine asters, delicate white orchids, golden yellow buttercups and
beautiful blue lupins all dance harmoniously in the sunlight.
Their sensational beauty is breathtaking and you walk the path
slowly with joy, savouring this moment.

The path through the meadow leads you into the cool pine
forest. The light is low here, and you can feel a more restful
atmosphere in the shelter of the trees.

You breathe in the forest atmosphere, feeling rejuvenated by the fresh, sharp, sweet smell of pine. Through the forest you reach the beginning of a mountain path.

As you walk, with your spine straight like a pine tree and your gaze steady, you feel the weight of your feet on the path. Notice how your weight is distributed left, right, front and back. You can feel the mountain supporting you, step by step.

Now, for the next few steps, stomp your feet firmly into the ground and swing your arms back and forth. Remain mindful and conscious as you do this. Releasing energy from your body and giving it back to the earth. A few steps will be sufficient, but you are welcome to do more if it feels good, as long as you remain intentional.

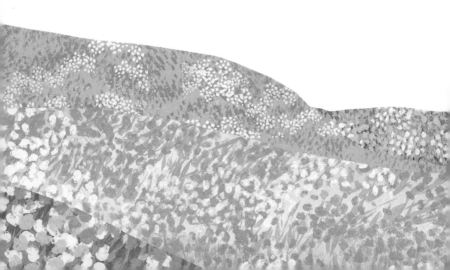

As you continue to walk along the mountain path, take a deep breath of pure, fresh air and begin to inhale from the soles of your feet, drawing energy up from the mountain all the way to the crown of your head.

Repeat this three or four times, embodying the mountain with every breath, feeling strong, rooted and unwavering.

You feel at peace, knowing that you can bring this grounding mountain energy into your life each and every day.

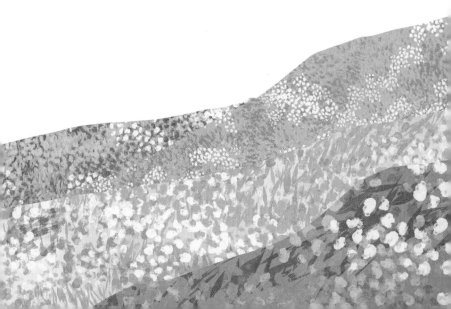

Connection

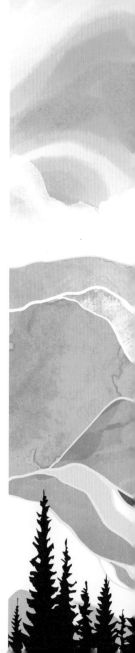

As you begin your walk, picture yourself walking on a cliff top at dawn. The sky is a vast, endless, deep purple, soft like velvet. The sea gently rocks back and forth, as the last stars fade away.

You smell crisp salt in the air and feel the soft cushion of grass underfoot as you walk. The special stillness before day breaks envelops you; it is a moment filled with peace and possibility.

Check in and notice how you feel in this moment. Bring your full attention to your body as it connects to the stillness within you.

Notice that from this place of connection and stillness a natural energy rises, just as the sun rises every day.

You look out to the horizon and see the new day beginning to dawn. Slowly, the darkness disappears and deep purple changes to violet and indigo tinged with pink, red and golden orange, as the sun begins to emerge from the water and the first rays of light touch your skin while you walk. You pause in awe to admire the wonder of it.

Check in and notice how you feel in this moment. Bring your full attention to your body. Feel the aliveness in every cell.

Notice from this place of connection and stillness that the mind becomes clearer and more receptive.

Picking up the pace, you retrace your steps along the cliff path. Walking with intention and clarity as the sun rises into the sky.

A remembering resides deep within, that just as day and night are connected, so are heaven and earth. You are not separate; you are a part of it. You can trust life to be just as it is.

Love

There are two paths: one is fear and the other is love.
As you walk, set your intention to be loving. There is
nothing to fear here.

Let your mind be light by softening
your brow and remind yourself
that being loving is a natural and
easy thing to do.

Smile slightly, breathe and, with your next out-breath, relax and soften your whole body. With every step you take, remind yourself that you are safe and that love strengthens and protects you.

On the next inhale, focus on deliberately sending your breath towards your heart. Inhale and direct the breath towards your heart, then follow this with an easy exhale. Repeat this a few times and, if it helps you to connect, place your hand on your heart as you do this.

As you breathe, become aware of any outer layers of protection your heart may have. These layers can build up at times of fear, heartbreak or emotional stress, so treat them with great tenderness and compassion as you meet them.

Notice the colour, texture and weight of these protective layers, and if you want to, you can allow any of these layers to dissolve with each exhale. As the layers dissolve, visualize the outer heart now protected by a soft, shimmering, green light.

On the next inhale, gently relax your heart. Take your time, telling yourself it is safe to relax your heart. Turn your attention to your inner heart, saying 'yes' to your heart and the love within it.

Visualize your inner heart filled with a soft, shimmering, pink light and let the love in your heart gently swell and expand.

Return your attention to your breath. On the next inhale, breathe love in and breathe love out. Repeat for a few cycles of breath and enjoy this moment to the fullest.

To complete this walking meditation, silently repeat the words: 'I am worthy, I am enough' three times to yourself.

If you need to, create a safe, nurturing space for yourself and be gentle with your heart throughout the rest of the day.

Appreciation

Release the need to control any outcomes in this moment. As you walk, feel or imagine the sunlight warming your skin and let your stress and tension melt away with every step you take. The warmth of the sun feels pleasurable on your face and body, and you feel at ease as you walk.

Notice the light and shade the sun produces all around you. Spend some time enjoying beautiful beams of sunlight creating sparkles and shadows that dance all around you.

Become aware that you are not just an observer of this experience; you are a part of it. Part of the whole – you belong here, right now in this moment.

Now imagine drawing the warmth of the sun into your chest and smiling as yellow and orange rays of light permeate your skin.

Feel the sensation as warm sunlight gently flows into your chest.

Expand the yellow and orange light in your chest now, so that it becomes a golden liquid light. Willingly accept the warmth of the sun as it fills you up with this golden liquid light, circulating your entire body, nourishing you and strengthening you from within.

Feel the sunlight pulsate in your body in sync with your footsteps and breathing. Enjoy this moment, drinking in the lifegiving force of the sun, step by step, breath by breath.

As you walk, stand a little taller and straighter, strengthened from within. You feel confident that you can shine your inner light out into the world.

Your inner light softly glows, emanating from your body as you walk. From this place of strength and light, you begin to appreciate yourself more deeply. Your qualities and quirks. Your struggles and your triumphs.

You feel appreciation for the world around you and the people you journey with each and every day; those you know and those you don't.

You have an appreciation for the sparkles and the shadows in life, knowing that the sun's light casts both and that both are needed for harmony and balance.

Say your name silently to yourself and give thanks to you for all that you are and all that you bring. Surround yourself in a bubble of protective yellow light and take this positive appreciation for yourself and others into the rest of your day.

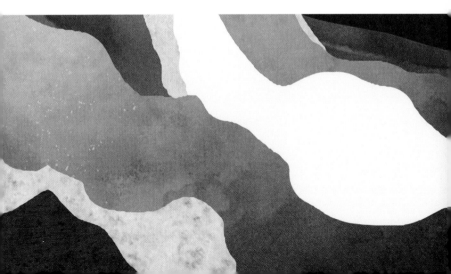

Purpose

Walking with a sense of purpose, you picture yourself following the bank of a twisting river that carved its path through the earth long, long ago.

The river is strong and clear and runs in one direction towards the ocean, flowing through fertile lands along the way to reach its destination. Its constant flow moves with quiet determination, always flowing forwards. Time is timeless to the river; there is no hurry here.

As you walk alongside the cool, clear waters, you draw strength from the river. You begin to think about your own life and all

your achievements so far. You acknowledge your successes
and those who helped you to rise up along the way.

Your attention shifts from your achievements and you begin
to ask yourself 'why?'

Why has your river of life flowed in this direction?

Why have you been called to make this particular journey
at this time?

Why are you here?

You let your thoughts meander gently, conceding that it may not yet be time for you to know all the answers, but, like the river, there is no hurry. Eventually, we all find our truth.

The river winds its way like a silver thread into the distance, and you begin to shift your thoughts to the future. You begin to imagine the next chapter of your own journey and how you want to be in your life moving forwards.

What kind of person would you like to be?

What qualities would you like to shine?

Keep this simple and, if possible, think of one or two words that sum up who you want to be moving forwards. Say the words to yourself over and over again, embedding them into the core of your being.

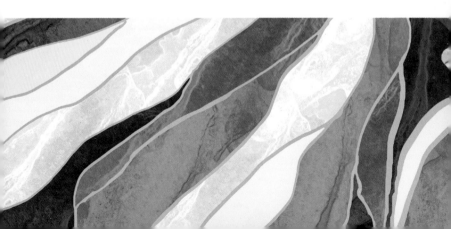

Know that this is why you are here –
this is your purpose. Trust that this is
who you are and believe in what you
are capable of.

Enjoy this moment to the fullest. Feel the forward momentum
you make with every step you take. Live your purpose, pursue
your dreams and, like the river, keep steadily moving forward.

Eventually, the river becomes one with the ocean. The ocean
becomes the rain and, as it rains, you can let go of everything
you have been thinking of now. Releasing all of your thoughts
and feelings, giving them all back to the earth. Trusting, like
the river, that you will naturally carve your path over time.

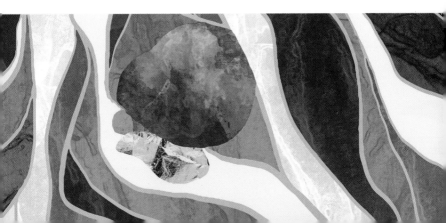

Part 3
Deeper Meditations

Introduction

These deeper meditations provide guidance for those times when you are feeling intense and difficult emotions such as grief, sorrow, fear, hurt, pain or anger.

You will be invited to follow a three- or four-step process, and some of these meditations also begin before you leave the house. Try not to skip any of the steps, as the whole process is designed to take you on a deeper journey into healing. Optional steps have been clearly marked and these may require more practise to ensure you feel ready to embrace them fully.

Always go at your own pace, and remember that you are in charge of how deep you want to go in your own process.

Comfort

RAIN is a Buddhist mindfulness tool that you can use to bring you comfort when feeling sorrow and grief. RAIN stands for:

Recognize

Allow

Investigate

Nurture

Step 1 Find comfort in the rhythm of your steps as your feet connect with the ground beneath you. Know you can come back to this rhythm at any time during your walking meditation. Begin to attune to a loss. This can be a loss you have experienced, a loss that touched you in the past, or a loss that you are anticipating. Recognize this loss and all that it means to you.

Step 2 Allow yourself to acknowledge the feelings associated with this loss. Let your feelings surface and be present. Deepen your awareness of how you are feeling with curiosity and care. Relax any resistance and be with your experience just as it is.

Step 3 As you continue to walk, focus on the rhythm of your breathing, the inhale and exhale. Now go a little deeper and begin to investigate – what are you telling yourself about this loss? What beliefs are you holding about this loss? Remain in a loving position towards yourself as you investigate.

Step 4 Now call on your higher self, an ancestor or a spiritual guide to give your heart the nurture and wisdom that is needed in this moment. Draw on the acceptance and love that comes from this higher source. Bathe in the caring presence that your heart deserves, feeling comforted that you are supported and guided.

Optional: If you are finding it difficult to release suffering, or to forgive yourself, imagine some clouds gathering overhead. The sky above becomes blanketed in a soft grey and you become aware of a raindrop lightly touching your cheek. You pause and look up to the sky, closing your eyes, as the soft, gentle rain washes away any pain you feel. You feel the cleansing rain releasing suffering and providing you with all the comfort and acceptance you need for your onward journey in life.

Compassion

Use this walking meditation when you have been hurt or are being hard on yourself.

Step 1 Before you leave, you are going to complete two exercises. The first is to write 'Who Am I?' at the top of a piece of paper. Write your responses on the page, taking time to reflect on your answers. If you get stuck, pause and come back to the question.

Step 2 Now sit in a comfortable, relaxed position. Spine straight, chin gently tipped towards your chest and eyes closed or gaze lowered. Take a breath and use the breath to clear your mind. Ask yourself 'Who Am I?' and allow an image to come to mind. Let the image come without trying to change it or alter it. Let the details emerge without needing to make sense of it. When you are ready, open your eyes and write about what you saw in as much detail as possible. Include how you felt and what the image meant to you.

Step 3 You are now ready to walk. As you walk, ask yourself 'Who Am I?' Allow the answers to be expressed through the movement of your body. Let the body and movement guide your responses. Trust the wisdom of your mind and body and keep walking until you experience a sense of wholeness again or you feel complete. If you are in a place where you feel comfortable, some of your expression may come through sound, words, tones or song. Feel free to express your full and true self!

Optional: On your return, you can write about your experience and share your discoveries with someone you trust, perhaps a close friend or family member, or a counsellor or therapist.

Note: Repeated use of this meditation process is highly recommended, as your insights will get deeper with practice.

Serenity

This meditation is designed to support you in expressing anger safely, so that you can return to a place of serenity.

Step 1 Find a safe place at home where you won't be disturbed for a few minutes. Stand with your feet about a hip-width apart. Locate the anger in your body and picture the person, organization or situation that caused it. Take a deep breath and, drawing on the inner strength and energy of a warrior, vigorously shake your arms for as long as you need to, to release the anger. Pause, breathe if you need to rest, and then begin again if you have more anger to release. Stay in the energy of a warrior without collapsing into other emotions.

Step 2 Find a different place to stand in the room, moving out of the place where you released your anger. Return to your original stance, arms relaxed by your sides, and focus on steady, even breaths. Assume a state of peace and relaxation. When you feel that you are back to a balanced state, you are ready to go for a walk.

Step 3 Take some time as you walk to think about the idea of serenity, holding it in your mind and reflecting on what it means to you. Now bring into your mind an image that represents serenity to you. Let the picture become clear with as much detail as you want to imagine with every step. Ask yourself, 'What is it about this place that feels serene? What benefits does serenity give me?'

Step 4 Begin to embody serenity as you walk. Relaxing your mind, your muscles and any tension. Let serenity be expressed in your face and repeat the word 'serenity' silently to yourself ten times, letting it permeate your being. Now experiment with radiating serenity out into the world, step by step, breath by breath.

Optional: Bring back into your mind the experience that you were angry about. See this person, organization or situation from your position of serenity. Knowing that you can do what is needed to protect yourself, look after yourself and take care of yourself. How could you respond from this place of serenity? What options are now available to you?

Part 4
Seasonal Meditations

Introduction

The seasons provide us with a constant natural rhythm. The longer walking meditations in this section are designed to help you reconnect with the rhythms of nature and develop a deeper awareness of your own cycles, so that you can work in harmony with them.

Each season embraces us with its energy in a different way. Spring invigorates us and invites us to use the healing and wisdom we gained from the depths of winter to express our deepest wishes and to step forward and claim what is fresh and new in our lives. Wisdom is said to be the integration of head and heart, so pay attention to both as you are walking.

Summer is a time of bounty and abundance, where the solar energy peaks and our own inner fire is stoked. In ancient times, people spent some of their day sleeping, so they could be awake during the night. This meant they received a balance of both sunlight and moonlight. Today, with our 9–5 work culture, we are less in harmony with these natural rhythms, but it is possible to bring moon bathing back into our lives by walking in the moonlight.

In traditional Chinese medicine, there is a short fifth season known as late summer. It is a subtle, separate season that occurs in late August and lasts until the autumn equinox in September (in the Northern Hemisphere), sometimes referred to in the West as an 'Indian Summer'. In the Chinese calendar, it marks the middle of the year, the point of transition from the expansion and growth of spring and summer (yang energy) and the more inward energy of autumn and winter (yin energy). Late summer is considered to be a place of balance, a time when everything comes back to the core. It's the perfect moment to use your walks to pause and reflect, so you can recentre, ground yourself and rebalance before autumn sweeps you back into its powerful energy of transition and change.

As the darkness of winter draws in, it is natural to slow down and turn inwards. At this time of year, yin energy increases and we become less active. As this stillness increases, you can use your walks as a time for reflection and introspection. Winter, if we wish to move through it, provides a doorway into our intuition and the mystery and magic of the deeper recesses of our being…

Spring

If you can, take this walk in the morning, perhaps even at sunrise when the outside world will be a little stiller for your moment of contemplation. Give yourself at least 30 minutes to enjoy this walk.

As you walk, picture in your mind's eye a walkway lined on both sides with cherry trees in full blossom. While you move along the walkway, your heart expands as you notice how each minute and perfectly formed petal plays its part in this joyous spectacle. Admire how each delicate blossom is perfectly formed, with pale pink petals and fine yellow stamens. Let your heart be filled with joy at nature's gift.

As you walk, expand this joy in your heart, step by step, breath by breath. Feel the joy spreading like a gentle, pale pink light from your heart into your chest and throat.

Now become aware of joy spreading from your chest down your arms, all the way to the tips of your fingers.

From your throat the joy runs gently down your spine, a delicate, pale pink light bathing your spine, vertebrae by vertebrae.

The pale pink light flows gently through both legs now, as your whole body is bathed in the soft warmth of joy.

Now imagine you are a cherry tree with deep roots and, with each step you take, send the energy of your roots deep into the earth beneath you. Purposefully channel your energy down into your roots, knowing it is these deep roots that allow for the growth of new branches.

Begin to draw up the powerful earth energy from your roots – with every step you take feeling the energy of the earth moving through your feet as you draw it up from your roots, through your legs and into your belly. Feeling this powerful earth energy as it nourishes and energizes you right at the core of your being.

From the core of you, this place of strength, which is supported by deep roots, imagine putting all your energy into something that you would love to blossom at this time. What would it be?

Bring into focus what it is you want to blossom.

What would happen if you gave it your all? How would putting your energy into this help you to grow physically, mentally or spiritually as a person?

Return to the walkway lined with cherry trees in your mind's eye. Watch as the petals fall softly like pale pink snowflakes.

As the beautiful blossoms fall onto the top of your head, touching your face and shoulders, you are reminded not to hold on too tightly to any of your plans, but simply to allow them to unfold naturally in the same way nature does every season.

Summer

This is an evening walk, which can be done before you go to bed. For maximum benefit, allow 30 minutes for this walk. This has the added advantage of disconnecting you from technology before you go to sleep, so that you can support and maintain balanced circadian rhythms as you prepare for sleep.

If you wish, you can schedule the full and super moons into your diary and take your walk during these times, when the moon's beams are even more potent. If it is appropriate to the place you decide to walk in, you could consider walking barefoot to maintain a strong connection to the earth while gazing at the celestial moon.

As you walk, focus your attention on the moon, if it is safe to do so; if not, you will still gain the benefits of this practice, even if you are unable to look directly at the moon.

Focus on your breathing as you walk and, on the inhale, breathe in the energy and light of the moon.

Let the luminosity of the moon bathe your whole body. Breathing in the pure golden light of the moon.

On the exhale, breathe out any areas of darkness or tension in your mind or body. Repeat this for as long as you want to, step by step, breath by breath.

Now pause, stand in your personal power and take this moment to fully appreciate the moon. Become aware of any reactions, responses or feelings that arise within you.

Breathe in the golden luminosity of the moon, then offer any of your reactions back to the moon. Allow your breathing to be easy and relaxed as you develop a symbiotic relationship with the moon, breathing in moonlight and offering back your response on the out-breath. Repeat this for as long as you want to.

Now, as you are standing in full appreciation of the moon, raise your arms up in a 'V' shape above your head. Let your heart open and take a deep breath, fully allowing the moon's beams to permeate every cell of your being. Reaching up to the light and letting the light in.

When you are complete and ready to return home, bring yourself back to your own inner wisdom. Consider how you are on your walk back, paying attention to your physical, mental and emotional experience.

Note: If you want to moon bathe at other times of the year, you can, of course, do that. If the weather is too cold or wet, you can stay indoors. Switch off the lights and lie down quietly in a place by a window that allows the moonlight to pour in and practise your appreciation of the moon, allowing the moon's light to brighten the dark spots within. If it is possible and comfortable, you could sleep in that place for the night and let your dreams be illuminated by the moon.

Late summer

This simple walking meditation is designed to help you slow down and celebrate your accomplishments. You could walk with a friend and have this experience as a conversation, if that feels good to you. If you do this, practise giving your full attention and listening to one another without comment or interruption. As one of you finishes speaking, that is the perfect moment to share your praise, admiration and acknowledgement for the other person's achievements.

Allow 60 minutes for this walk and talk, if you can, so that both of you have plenty of space and time to do so. You can turn around after 30 minutes and switch over at this halfway point. As you walk, consider (or share) the following thoughts:

- Where can you most see the positive fruits of your labours this year?
- What has it taken from you to accomplish this?
- What are you most proud of?
- How have you celebrated this?

When you get home, you may want to write your reflections down in a journal to create a place you can return to and remember in the depths of winter, or when you are sowing fresh seeds in spring.

Autumn

As you begin to walk, bring your
shoulders up to your ears for one deep
inhale and then release your shoulders
on the exhale. Repeat twice more, and
if you're able to make an 'ahhh' sound
on the exhale, even better.

Now pay particular attention to the back
of your body, focusing on your spine
being strong and straight. With your next
inhale, draw the breath in through your
nose and up into your head, then imagine
your breath falling like golden rain down
your spine, vertebrae by vertebrae, with an
easy exhale out through your open mouth.

Repeat two or three times, maintaining
a strong back bone; your body and breath
are easy and relaxed as you take each step.

On the next inhale, pay attention to the front of your body. With each breath, gradually follow your breath down through your throat and into your chest until eventually your breath reaches your belly. Take your time and allow the rhythm of your steps to assist your breathing to become full and deep.

As your breath begins to reach your belly, imagine a small, golden orange glow forming in your belly.

Visualize this golden orange glow and watch it expand to become refined orange light.

This clear orange light begins to spin, gently to start with, as you move your attention to this wheel of light. Watch the direction the glow spins in – is it spinning clockwise or anticlockwise?

Either way, it is okay. Breathe deeply into the light and, with every breath, let the light expand, making the wheel brighter and more vivid.

Take your time. Observe. Trust.

Now spin the wheel of orange light in the opposite direction. As you do this, notice whether it has a temperature. Can you feel its warmth or coolness? Expand the light with each breath. Notice any changes to the temperature if they occur.

Take your time. Observe. Trust.

As you connect with the light, let it spin in any direction. As it spins, ask to be shown a symbol, image or word that would support you in your life at this time.

Take your time. Observe. Trust.

When you are ready, place your right hand on your belly and your left hand over your right, then repeat silently to yourself three times: 'I feel at peace. I am in the right place.'

Now take a slow inhale and an easy exhale, then watch as the wheel dissolves and the orange light permeates the cells of your being. Use your hands to envelope yourself in a lustrous, protective bubble of orange light to complete this experience.

Winter

As you walk, signal to your mind and body that you are going on an inner journey by following your breath in through your nose and out through your mouth for five breath cycles.

Now, in your mind's eye, picture yourself walking out towards a remote, wild Icelandic glacier. The sun slowly creeps over the ocean horizon, as your feet crunch on the rocky ground beneath you, and imposing black mountains tower above you, casting long shadows as you walk.

As you continue to walk, you reach an enormous expanse of brilliant blue-white ice. It stretches as far as the eye can see, and you are in awe of the power and majesty of this water, which has been frozen in time, weathering seasons and storms for tens of thousands of years.

In front of you there is a tunnel, a doorway formed by the forces of nature, which, if you choose to enter, will take you into caves deep beneath the glacier.

You choose to enter the tunnel and, as you do so, you reflect on the difficult terrain you have had to traverse during your own life. You consider the twists and turns, the challenges along the way.

You reflect on your own behaviours with truth and love. Where could you have responded differently? What stopped you at the time?

As you continue to walk, you reflect on the behaviours of others during these difficult times, again with compassion and kindness. Where could they have responded differently? What do you imagine stopped them at that time?

Walking through the dark tunnel deep beneath the glacier, you let yourself reflect on the darkest recesses of your own being. The places you have kept hidden even from yourself. You do this with as much love for yourself as you can muster.

As you go even deeper, you realize that these experiences are nothing to be ashamed of and, one by one, you begin to forgive yourself or others for any hurt that was caused. You understand that now is the time to let go, and you are able to find forgiveness with ease in your heart.

As you let go, you turn a corner in the darkness and enter a magnificent chamber illuminated with a deep blue glow. Looking up, you see a roof of ice above you; it looks as if a vibrant turquoise river is flowing overhead.

As the sun shines through the ice roof, the inner glacier is transformed into an exquisite sapphire ice cave.

The light reflects blues so deep that they are almost violet, and you see there is extraordinary beauty even when something has been frozen in time.

The grandeur is breathtaking and you are mesmerized by the vibrancy of this extraordinary other world. Like your own inner ocean, you understand there is much to be discovered here and that you can return at any time.

About the author

Danielle North has worked with senior leaders globally for two decades. She is the founder of Pause Global, a talent development consultancy that takes a unique but simple approach: if you're going to perform in a world that's speeding up, sometimes you need to slow down. Partnering with HR and talent teams around the world, Pause addresses the challenges people face, from stress management and burnout to career performance and personal transformation.

A speaker and four times published author, Danielle's books have collectively sold over 60,000 copies and been translated into more than 10 languages.

www.pauseglobal.com

@pause.global